CENTER FIELD

The History of Baseball

JAIME WINTERS

CRABTREE
Publishing Company
www.crabtreebooks.com

Author: Jaime Winters

Editors: Marcia Abramson, Kelly Spence

Proofreader: Jillian Harvey

Photo research: Melissa McClellan

Design: T. J. Choleva

Cover design: Samara Parent

Prepress technician: Samara Parent

Production coordinator: Margaret Amy Salter

Consultant: James L. Gates Jr., Library Director
National Baseball Hall of Fame and Museum

Produced for Crabtree Publishing
by BlueApple*Works* Inc.

Front Cover:
Background image: Players in the 1937 All-Star
Game. Left to right: Lou Gehrig, Joe Cronin, Bill
Dickey, Joe DiMaggio, Charlie Gehringer, Jimmie
Foxx, and Hank Greenberg

Inset Right: Moses Fleetwood Walker played with
the Major League team Toledo Blue Stockings
until baseball's color barrier was enforced

Inset Left: Pitching great Cy Young of the
Cleveland Naps

Title Page: Jackie Robinson

Photographs
Front Cover: Library of Congress: Harris & Ewing collection (background); Public Domain (inset left); Wikimedia Commons: Public Domain American Tobacco Company (inset right) Shutterstock: (bottom right)
Interior: Corbis: © Bettmann/Corbis (p 19 right); © Layne Kennedy/Corbis (p 25) Shutterstock.com: © Mike Flippo (TOC top); © James R. Martin (TOC background); © Ben Carlson (chapter page topper); © David Lee (page toppers); © Africa Studio (baseball); © Patricia Hofmeester (p 7 left); © elvisvaughn (p 9 left); © Debby Wong (p 9, p 16 top); © Photo Works (p 17 left); © Aspen Photo (p 17 middle); © Sean Pavone (p 26–27 top); © gary yim (p26–27 bottom); © Joyce Vincent (p 26 left); © Alan C. Heison (p 28) Keystone Press: © Jose Luis Villegas (p 27 left); © Aflo (p 27 right); © Josie Lepe (p 29 top); © Josie Lepe (p 29 bottom)
Library of Congress: National Photo Company Collection (p 5 top, 21 top right); Joseph Boggs Beale (p 6–7 top); Dorothea Lange (p 6 bottom); L. Prang & Co. (p 7 top); Valadon & Cie Boussod (p 7 bottom); Arthur Rothstein (p 7 right, p 9 right); FSA/OWI Collection (p 11 top); Sarony, Major & Knapp (p 11 bottom); Bain News Service (p 12–13 top, p 15 left, p 17 far left, p 20 left); Pictorial News Co. (p 12–13 bottom); Charles H. Williamson (p 12 right); George Grantham Bain Collection (p 13 left), p 14); Tuchfarber, Walkley & Moellmann (p 15 right); Harris & Ewing (p 17 right, p 22, p 23 bottom); Gladstone collection (p 18–19 bottom); R.W. Johnston Studios (p 20–21 top); F.A. Flowers Co. (p 20–21 bottom); Harris & Ewing (p 21 left); The Sporting News Pub (p 23 top)
Library and Archives Canada: Ronny Jaques/Library and Archives Canada/PA (title page); Canada. Dept. of National Defence/Library and Archives Canada/PA-035767 (p 6); Thinkstock: © Thinkstock (16 left); © Fuse (p 30)
Public Domain: (p 4 left); John F Shale (p 4 right, p 6 left); James J. Williams (p 8); Charles H. Williamson (p 9 top); Currier & Ives (p 10); Gray (p 12 left, p 13 right, p 19 top); State Library and Archives of Florida (p 24)
Creative Commons: Bundesarchiv, Bild 10 (p 5 bottom)

Library and Archives Canada Cataloguing in Publication

Winters, Jaime, author
    Center field : the history of baseball / Jaime Winters.

(Baseball source)
Includes index.
Issued in print and electronic formats.
ISBN 978-0-7787-1476-7 (bound).--ISBN 978-0-7787-1867-3 (pbk.).--
ISBN 978-1-4271-7617-2 (pdf).--ISBN 978-1-4271-7613-4 (html)

    1. Baseball--History--Juvenile literature. I. Title. II. Title: History of baseball.

GV862.5.W56 2015   j796.357   C2014-908291-6
                                          C2014-908292-4

Library of Congress Cataloging-in-Publication Data

Winters, Jaime.
  Center field : the history of baseball / Jaime Winters.
    pages cm. -- (Baseball Source)
  Includes index.
  ISBN 978-0-7787-1476-7 (reinforced library binding : alk. paper) --
  ISBN 978-0-7787-1867-3 (paperback : alk. paper) --
  ISBN 978-1-4271-7617-2 (electronic PDF) --
  ISBN 978-1-4271-7613-4 (electronic HTML)
  1. Baseball--History--Juvenile literature. I. Title.

  GV867.5.W56 2015
  796.357--dc23
                                2014048909

Crabtree Publishing Company

www.crabtreebooks.com   1-800-387-7650

Printed in Canada/042015/BF20150203

Published in Canada
Crabtree Publishing
616 Welland Ave.
St. Catharines, ON
L2M 5V6

Published in the United States
Crabtree Publishing
PMB 59051
350 Fifth Avenue, 59th Floor
New York, New York 10118

Published in the United Kingdom
Crabtree Publishing
Maritime House
Basin Road North, Hove
BN41 1WR

Published in Australia
Crabtree Publishing
3 Charles Street
Coburg North
VIC 3058

CONTENTS

LET'S PLAY BALL!

ANCIENT BATTERS

Who invented baseball? No one knows exactly when and where the game started. Long ago, ancient Egyptians, Greeks, Persians, and Native Nations of North America all played games with bats and balls.

Rounders and Cricket

By the 1100s, Europeans were playing bat-and-ball games. These games developed into cricket and rounders. In cricket, players bat the ball and run end to end to score. In rounders, a batter hits a ball thrown by a pitcher and runs around posts. The opposing team then tries to hit the batter with the ball to get the batter "out."

Rounders has been played since the 1500s. This picture shows a game being played in 1913. Kids still play rounders today in the United Kingdom.

Cricket's history dates back to the sixteenth century. By 1800, it had spread over England. This picture shows a game in 1817.

Russian Baseball?

Archeologists have uncovered bats and balls in Novgorod, one of Russia's oldest cities. The artifacts show that lapta, a game much like baseball, was played there during the 1300s. Lapta is still played in Russia today. Teams have six players each. A server bats a ball to a batter. Batters aim to hit the ball over a 33-foot (10-m) line. Teammates then try to score by running to an end line and back before the server's team pelts them with the ball.

OFF THE BAT!

The oldest-known record of a game more similar to baseball than rounders appeared in *Boy's Own Book* in 1829. The game was called "Round Ball," "Base," and "Goal Ball."

*European stick-and-ball games came to America along with **immigrant** families.*

German Schlagball

By the 1700s, Germans were playing schlagball, a game like rounders. In German, schlagball means "hit the ball." Teams had 12 players a side. Players pitched and hit the ball and runners ran around a group of bases.

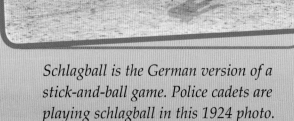

Schlagball is the German version of a stick-and-ball game. Police cadets are playing schlagball in this 1924 photo.

5

HUMBLE BEGINNINGS

In the 1700s, English settlers came to North America and brought the games they loved with them. Cricket didn't catch on. It could take days to play and was seen as a game for the wealthy. But rounders became popular.

Rounders Rocks Out

Kids set up rocks, sticks, or stools for bases and began playing rounders in towns all over. In most games, a batter tried to hit a ball thrown by a pitcher and then run around the bases without being pounded out by the ball. The name of the game varied from town to town—it was called town ball, round ball, sting ball, burn ball, soak ball, stool ball, and even base ball.

Town ball was played both in country pastures (left) and in clubs organized in towns.

Local Games, Local Rules

The rules of rounders also differed from town to town. The number of bases varied from two to five, along with the way they were laid out and the distance between them. Some towns had no teams, with just a batter playing against a mob of fielders. Others had batters try to hit a pitch that bounced off a barn wall. Town teams **evolved** as the game spread across the country.

People all over North America played town ball—including future U.S. president Abraham Lincoln.

The Ball: Then and Now

Players made early balls from whatever was on hand, such as a walnut wrapped in an old sock. The balls quickly turned soft and mushy. Soon, players began winding yarn around rubber and covering it in leather to make balls that lasted longer and traveled farther. Today, balls have a cork core wrapped in layers of rubber, wool, and cotton covered with hand-stitched leather.

Early baseballs came in different sizes and shapes because they were handmade. The first baseball factory opened in 1858.

7

FATHERS OF BASEBALL

Rounders and its many spinoffs were kids' games. But when a few adults began tinkering with the rules of the game in the 1800s, everything changed.

The Rule Maker

In 1845, a 25-year-old bank teller named Alexander J. Cartwright started the Knickerbocker Base Ball Club of New York. Each week, Cartwright brought new rules for the club to try out at the **vacant** lot where they met. He chose the rules from different versions of the game and added his own ideas, too. Cartwright decided to use four bases set in a diamond shape and allowed pitchers to throw overhand rather than just underhand. Instead of beaning runners with the ball for an "out," Cartwright had fielders "tag" them with the ball. He wrote down the rules and modern baseball was born.

Alexander J. Cartwright was honored by both the Baseball Hall of Fame and the United States Congress as the inventor of modern baseball.

The First Shortstop

Daniel "Doc" Adams began playing baseball for exercise in 1839. The young medical doctor soon joined the Knickerbocker Base Ball Club. He noticed that outfielders often had difficulty throwing the ball to infielders. So he began playing **shortstop** by throwing the ball from outfielders to infielders. This closed up a big gap on the field and became a regular position. Adams also designed bats and balls to improve their performance and helped establish the rules of the game.

Daniel Adams (center) was a team leader of the New York Knickerbockers from 1846 to 1862. The team played so well that other baseball clubs modeled themselves after the team.

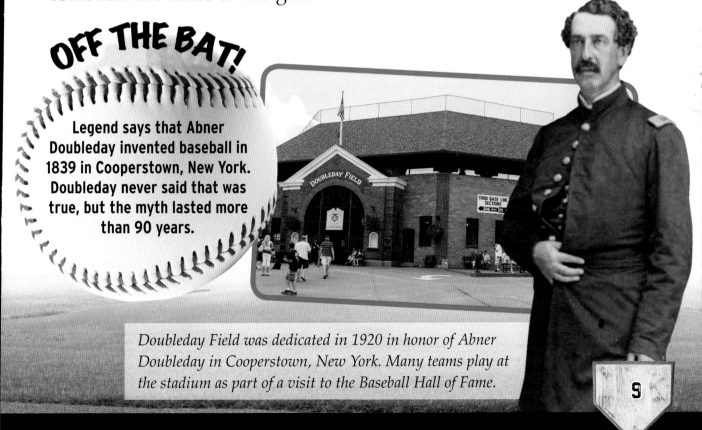

OFF THE BAT!

Legend says that Abner Doubleday invented baseball in 1839 in Cooperstown, New York. Doubleday never said that was true, but the myth lasted more than 90 years.

Doubleday Field was dedicated in 1920 in honor of Abner Doubleday in Cooperstown, New York. Many teams play at the stadium as part of a visit to the Baseball Hall of Fame.

9

THE NEW YORK RULES

Alexander J. Cartwright's rules turned what had been a kids' game to pass the time into a complex and exciting sport. Adults began to play baseball and the game spread across North America like wildfire.

Game Catches On

The Knickerbocker Base Ball Club of New York adopted Cartwright's rules in 1845. Not only did the rules make the game more exciting but they also **standardized** plays and the size and shape of the field. The acceptance of a standardized set of rules by different clubs meant that competitive leagues could be formed. The appearance of leagues allowed for the growth of championship series, and the popularity of the game took off.

New York City was growing big and crowded, so the Knickerbockers played their games at the Elysian Fields in nearby Hoboken, New Jersey. Their first official game took place on June 19, 1846.

Baseball Fever

As clubs sprung up to challenge the Knickerbockers, baseball fever struck New York City. Huge crowds began gathering along the field to watch the action. In 1857, the Knickerbockers and more than 12 other clubs set up a rules committee and an all-star game.

Crowds have been packing baseball stadiums in the New York City area for more than 150 years.

Soon, they formed the National Association of Base Ball Players (NABBP) to govern the game. By 1859, baseball fever had also swept across the Canadian border.

War Boosts the Game

During the Civil War (1861–1865), Union soldiers from the northeast often played baseball to let off steam behind the **front**. Fellow soldiers and Confederate prisoners watched them and learned how to play.

Baseball was already being played in the southern states before the Civil War, but the returning soldiers playing on both sides helped popularize the game after the war.

Soldiers on both sides played baseball during the Civil War. Prisoners of war and even their guards played, too. A Union officer drew this picture of a game at a prison camp in North Carolina.

11

THE FIRST MAJOR LEAGUES

After the Civil War, the number of clubs in the NABBP shot up from a few dozen to about 100. A year later, over 200 teams had joined.

The Next Level

As fans turned up to games in record numbers and devoured news about their favorite players, baseball quickly became the all-American game. By 1869, people wanted to take the game to the next level. Many felt the NABBP wasn't up to the job. They felt it was not focused on the game beyond New York. They also felt its rule that baseball was only for **amateurs** and not **professionals** was outdated.

The Brooklyn Atlantics got their start in 1855 and quickly became one of baseball's top clubs. They turned pro as soon as it was allowed in 1869.

George Hall was one of many professional baseball players who played in the National Association and later the National League.

Big Bucks, Big Leagues

In 1871, nine clubs got together and formed the National Association of Professional Baseball Players. But the organization didn't last. As more and more fans paid cash for game tickets, club owners wanted in on the **profits**. They weren't happy with the National Association, where players made the rules and all the money. In 1876, several owners met behind closed doors and formed the National League to take control of the rules—and the profits. In 1900, the American League was started. In 1903, the first informal World Series was played, pitting the top team from each league against each other in a championship tournament. In 1905, the two leagues formalized the World Series as a league-approved annual postseason event.

The Boston Americans beat the Pittsburgh Pirates in the first World Series in 1903. Huge crowds watched as the new American League champions proved that they could play as well as the National League players.

Boston's Cy Young made the first pitch of the first World Series. His record of 511 career wins is still baseball's best. The Cy Young Award for pitching was named in his honor.

13

As major league baseball evolved, so did the game. Baseball players went from being amateur athletes to pros who were paid top dollar to play.

Pay for Play

Unlike pro athletes, amateurs are not paid to play sports. The Knickerbocker club stated baseball was for amateurs only and turned down offers to go pro. Nevertheless, many players were paid secretly or through **phony**, or fake, jobs. For example, in 1876, ace pitcher Al Spalding was offered a job in Chicago as a grocery store clerk for $40 per week. The pay was about 10 times higher than the regular wage of a grocery clerk. It was added motivation to play for Chicago.

OFF THE BAT!

Players on the New York Mutuals from 1861–1870 were put on the city payroll as "street sweepers" by a politician.

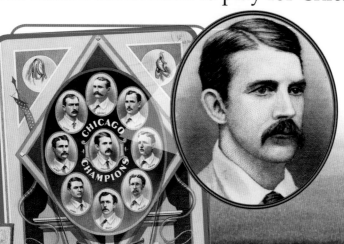

Al Spalding, a star pitcher for the Chicago White Stockings, was one of the first players to use a glove. He started a company to sell them. Spalding is still a big name in sports equipment.

First Pro Club

As more and more baseball clubs formed, competition for top players became extremely fierce. Every club wanted the best players and some were prepared to pay whatever it took. In 1869, the Cincinnati Red Stockings stacked their whole team with pro players and went on a cross-country tour. They took on any challengers, winning 56 games and tying one. Other clubs then signed pros. The game itself soon turned pro as amateur clubs could no longer sign top players who brought people out to the ball game.

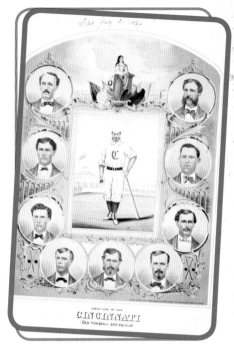

The Cincinnati Red Stockings started a baseball trend with their long socks and short pants. The socks were made by a young woman named Margaret Truman.

The Reserve Clause

How could cash-starved clubs stay competitive if rich clubs could lure their star players away with big bucks? In 1879, the National League created the reserve clause that allowed clubs to "reserve" players for the next season. Then other clubs couldn't sign those players. But the league didn't tell the players!

Fans would do anything, even climb lampposts, to see top players in action. Clubs kept stars from switching teams by using the reserve clause until it was abolished in 1975.

15

CHANGING EQUIPMENT

Over the years, hammering a home run, catching a fly ball, and fielding a **grounder** have not changed much. But the equipment players use to play the game sure has.

Batter Up!

When kids played rounders in the 1700s, they batted with whatever they could find. An old ax handle, broomstick, tree branch, or even the spoke of a wagon wheel would do. Today, players of all levels except Major League Baseball use aluminum bats, which last longer than wooden ones and almost never break. However, only solid wood bats are allowed in the major leagues.

Helmets Rule

Today, batters step up to the plate wearing strong, plastic helmets to protect their heads from wild pitches. However, batting helmets did not become required gear until 1971. Before that, players went to bat in the cloth cap they wore to keep the sun out of their eyes.

Batters had much less protection in the early days of baseball.

Catcher's Gear

The first catchers wore no protective gear at all. In the 1870s, catchers developed masks to shield their faces from the ball. A padded mitt followed around 1889 and shin guards around 1910. Today, catchers wear a full suit of armor: a mask, helmet, neck protector, throat guard, chest protector, shin guards, and a mitt with extra padding.

Catchers today have stronger and better equipment that helps them stay safe behind the plate.

Gloves

In 1875, Charles Waite played first base with flesh-colored gloves, hoping no one would notice. People did and they made fun of him. But not for long! Gloves became standard field equipment. Today, players use leather gloves with unique features to help them play their positions.

The first baseball gloves were made from leather work gloves. Players cut off the fingertips so they could control the ball.

17

AFRICAN AMERICAN PLAYERS

From 1887 to 1947, no African Americans or other players of color played major league baseball. Here's why.

No Blacks Allowed

In the late 1800s, **racism** was widespread across the United States. Many white people believed that black people were **inferior**, or second-class, to the white race. Laws were made that did not allow African Americans to work as firefighters, police officers, and schoolteachers, or go to school with whites. Though there was no rule in the rule book, African Americans were also shut out of major league baseball. In 1887, the New York Giants were interested in signing ace African American pitcher George Stovey. But when Chicago superstar Cap Anson protested, the Giants backed out. African Americans did not play in the big leagues for the next 60 years.

The Kansas City Monarchs and Hilldale, a Pennsylvania team, met in the first Negro World Series in 1924. The last one was played in 1948.

The Negro Leagues

But nothing would stop African Americans from playing baseball. In the northeast, amateur teams made up entirely of African American players had been around since the 1860s. Soon, all-black professional teams formed, which then led to the creation of the "Negro Leagues." The Negro Leagues had some of the game's best players. Catcher Josh Gibson racked up an incredible number of career home runs. Pitcher Leroy "Satchel" Paige often had his fielders sit down while he struck out three batters in a row. Once the color barrier came down in 1947, the Negro Leagues began to fold.

OFF THE BAT!

Before the unwritten color rule was enforced, catcher Moses Fleetwood Walker (above) and his brother played Major League Baseball for the Toledo Blue Stockings in 1884. After 1887, African Americans didn't play again in the big leagues until 1947, when Jackie Robinson smashed the rule for good.

Jackie Robinson led the way for African American players. He became the first black player in modern baseball on April 15, 1947, and went on to star for the Brooklyn Dodgers.

THE DEADBALL ERA

Ever tried to hit a ball that has no liveliness or bounce? If so, chances are it didn't travel very far. That's exactly what it's like to hit a deadball.

Pitchers Duel

In 1901, the ball was less lively than today. Also, it wasn't taken out of play after it turned soft and mushy. Add to that a new rule that counted foul balls as strikes, and the Deadball Era began. Suddenly pitchers could put away batters like never before. Strikeouts skyrocketed, hits plunged, and few runs were scored. Many games were low-scoring contests between pitchers. In 1910, the ball got livelier, but pitchers covered it with spit, Vaseline, and scratches to keep scores low. The Deadball Era didn't end until 1920, when spitballs, shine balls, and scuffballs were outlawed.

Sam Crawford played for Cincinnati and Detroit in the Deadball Era. That didn't stop the slugging outfielder from setting the career record for triples, 309, which still stands.

The Babe

From 1914 to 1935, George Herman "Babe" Ruth hit the ball out of the park a record-setting 714 times. People were stunned. The previous record holder of the most career home runs had been only 138. When Babe played for the Boston Red Sox from 1914 to 1919, he was the best left-handed pitcher around. With the "Bambino" on the team, the Red Sox won three World Series.

Babe Ruth started in baseball as a record-setting pitcher for the Red Sox, but he wanted to play every day and became an outfielder instead.

The arrival of Babe Ruth made the Yankees a powerhouse in baseball. He won four more World Series and set many hitting records as a Yankee.

OFF THE BAT!

People say the "Curse of the Bambino" fell on the Boston Red Sox in 1919, when they sold Babe Ruth to the New York Yankees. The Red Sox didn't win the World Series again for 86 years.

BASEBALL SOLDIERS ON

When the United States joined World War II in 1941, many baseball players **enlisted** in the army. How did the game go on without them? Read on to find out.

Keep It Going

The United States didn't make baseball players **exempt** from military service. But President Franklin D. Roosevelt said it was "best for the country to keep baseball going." He thought people would be working longer and harder and would need to take their minds off their work more than ever before. So the game went on with underage players, older players who came out of retirement, and players who were exempt from military service due to medical or physical conditions. A one-armed outfielder played 77 games for the St. Louis Browns!

Franklin D. Roosevelt, who was president during World War II, kept the tradition of throwing out a first pitch every season. Each president since 1910 has tossed at least one ceremonial first pitch.

Not the Same Game

Nothing was the same during the war—not the hits, not the pitching, not even the ball. Without the game's top players, the quality of play dropped. So did the quality of the ball. All the good yarn went into army blankets and other war items. The ball didn't travel as far then, and home runs became tougher to hit. But maybe that was good, as most pitchers didn't have the skill to stop batters from whacking the ball over the fence. In fact, clubs began using **relief pitchers** partway through games to try to fix their pitching difficulties.

Yankee slugger Joe DiMaggio kissed his bat after setting a major league record by getting a hit in 56 straight games in 1941. He kissed baseball good-bye, though, to serve in the Army Air Corps in World War II.

Four of these 1937 All-Stars later served in World War II. From left to right: Lou Gehrig, Joe Cronin, Bill Dickey, Joe DiMaggio, Charlie Gehringer, Jimmie Foxx, and Hank Greenberg.

Yankee great Lou Gehrig retired in 1939 due to a crippling condition called amyotrophic lateral sclerosis, or ALS. From then on, it also became known as Lou Gehrig's disease.

A LEAGUE OF THEIR OWN

By 1943, baseball's stars were missing in major league action due to World War II. Club owners were looking for a spark to bring fans back into the ballpark. So Chicago Cubs' owner Phil Wrigley decided to start a women's baseball league.

Women in Baseball

Women had been playing baseball since the game began. Wrigley began by launching a professional women's softball league. The rules were **tweaked** to give batters an edge over pitchers, and stealing bases was allowed. That way, big hits and exciting plays would hopefully draw fans to see rip-roaring games. And they did. About 200,000 spectators turned out to watch the games. In 1944, the league traded its softball for a hardball, gave pitchers the greenlight to throw the ball overhand, and changed its name to the All-American Girls Baseball League.

Dorothy "Dottie" Schroeder was only 15 when she became the youngest player in professional women's baseball. She played from 1943 through 1954.

Taking the Field Now

The All-American Girls Baseball League lasted until 1954. Today, women and girls continue to play the game as well as teeball, softball, and fast-pitch softball. To date, no women play major league baseball in North America. However, in 2009, pitcher Eri Yoshida became the first woman to play pro ball in a men's league in Japan. And women continue to knock on major league baseball's door. In 2011, Justine Siegel pitched batting practice to six major league teams during spring training.

OFF THE BAT!

In 1998, Ila Borders became the first woman to win a men's pro baseball game. She pitched six shutout innings for the minor league Duluth-Superior Dukes of Minnesota to beat the Sioux Falls Canaries.

Ila Borders pitched in the minors from 1997 to 2000 and was the first woman to start a minor league game.

Take me out to the ball game! After World War II, fans flocked to ballparks in record numbers. From 1945–1949, attendance almost doubled from 10.8 million to 20 million.

The Game Grows

Even though the way the game was played hadn't changed much, baseball's popularity kept growing. In the 1950s, more people became baseball fans as games were broadcast on TV. In the 1960s, 10 new clubs bounced into the major leagues, and in the 1990s, four more rolled in. Today, games are broadcast on TV, radio, and the Internet. In 2013, Major League Baseball had the highest season attendance of sports leagues in the world, as more than 74 million people watched games.

*Enthusiastic fans support their teams when they buy game tickets, snacks, and souvenirs. Sales of advertising and **broadcast rights** also help teams make money.*

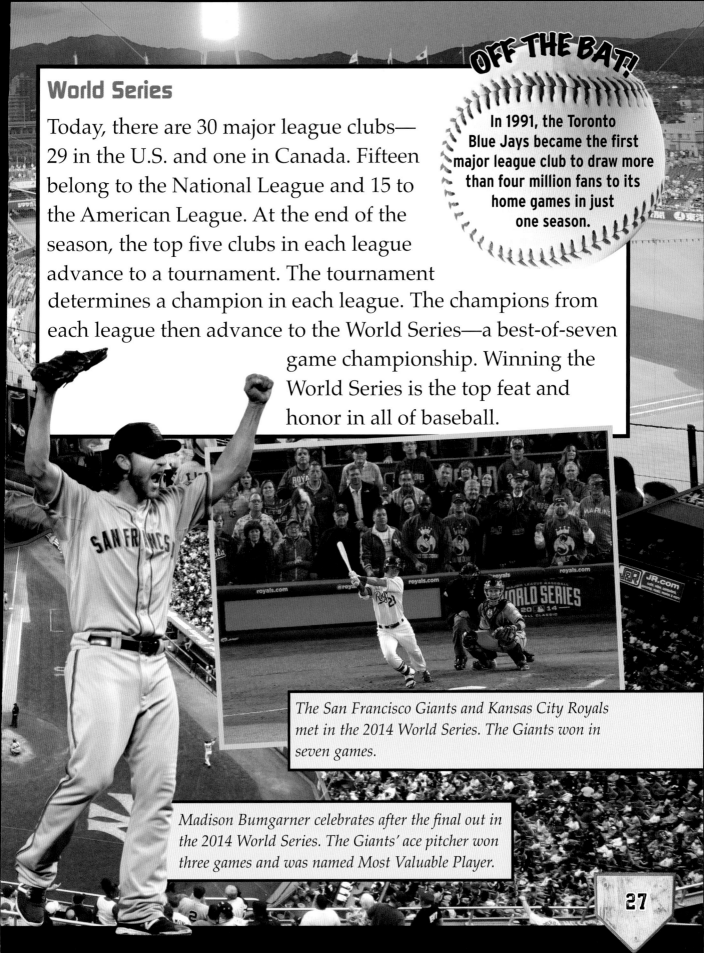

World Series

Today, there are 30 major league clubs—29 in the U.S. and one in Canada. Fifteen belong to the National League and 15 to the American League. At the end of the season, the top five clubs in each league advance to a tournament. The tournament determines a champion in each league. The champions from each league then advance to the World Series—a best-of-seven game championship. Winning the World Series is the top feat and honor in all of baseball.

OFF THE BAT!

In 1991, the Toronto Blue Jays became the first major league club to draw more than four million fans to its home games in just one season.

The San Francisco Giants and Kansas City Royals met in the 2014 World Series. The Giants won in seven games.

Madison Bumgarner celebrates after the final out in the 2014 World Series. The Giants' ace pitcher won three games and was named Most Valuable Player.

THE WORLD'S GAME

Once baseball fever hit North America, it wasn't long before countries around the world caught the baseball bug, too.

Have Game, Will Travel

As players traveled around the world, they took the game with them. Around 1872, American Horace Wilson was teaching in Japan. Wilson had played baseball, perhaps when he served in the U.S. Civil War. He thought his students needed some exercise away from their desks, so he taught them how to play baseball. The game caught on and a few years later Japan had its first ball team. In 1878, pro ball player Esteban Bellan took the game to Cuba, where it became a hit and spread throughout the Caribbean. Sailors of the U.S. Navy played an important role in spreading the game around the Caribbean as well. In 1888, games were played in Australia, New Zealand, and the South Pacific. Today, Major League Baseball includes players that come from baseball hotspots around the world, such as Japan, Korea, Cuba, Mexico, Taiwan, Australia, and Canada.

Team Japan won the World Baseball Classic in 2006 and 2009 with players including MLB star Ichiro Suzuki.

World Baseball Classic

In 1938, the International Baseball Federation formed. The United States, Canada, Cuba, France, England, Hawaii (not yet a state), Mexico, Spain, Egypt, China, Japan, Peru, the Philippines, Belgium, the Netherlands, and Germany all soon joined. Today, more than 100 countries belong. Countries go to bat against each other in the World Baseball Classic held every four years. Countries' teams feature players from leagues around the world, including Major League Baseball.

The Dominican Republic swept the World Baseball Classic in 2013, winning all eight of its games.

After beating Puerto Rico, the Dominican Republic team celebrated its championship.

LET'S PLAY BALL

So, you want to get in the game? Whether you want to compete in a junior world series, become a future baseball superstar, or just play for fun, there are lots of opportunities to play ball!

Youth Baseball

Check out your local teeball team, Pony League™, softball league, or Little League®. Many leagues focus on giving kids a chance to play ball and develop the skills of batting, throwing, pitching, running, and catching.

Little League® World Series

If you want to cut your teeth in competition, there's always the Little League® World Series (LLWS). Every year, all-star teams of boys and girls from baseball and softball youth leagues around the world take to the field for the LLWS. The players on each team all come from the same league, and the action is often just as exciting as major league ball.

Millions of kids around the world love to play ball!

LEARNING MORE

Check out these books and websites to find out more about the game.

Books

Baseball: How It Works (The Science of Sports (Sports Illustrated for Kids)) by David Dreier, c. 2010, Capstone Press

The Best of Everything Baseball Book (The All-Time Best of Sports) by Nate LeBoutillier, c. 2011, Capstone Press

Baseball (DK Eyewitness Books) by James Buckley Jr., c. 2010, DK Publishing

Websites

Major League Baseball Kids
The MLB site for kids features photos, videos, and information about its special programs for kids.
www.mlb.com/mlb/kids/

Baseball Hall of Fame
The Baseball Hall of Fame has information about the history of baseball and the best baseball players of the past.

www.baseballhall.org

Little League® World Series
This site has information about the Little League® World Series.
www.llbws.org/home

GLOSSARY

Note: Some boldfaced words are defined where they appear in the book.

amateurs Athletes who don't get paid for playing sports

archeologists People who study ancient structures, tools, and relics

broadcast rights Legal rights to show events through radio or television

enlisted Joined or signed up for, especially used for military service

evolved Changed over time

exempt Not required to do something or obey a rule that others must follow

front In a war, the area where opposing forces are fighting close together

grounder A batted baseball that rolls or bounces along the ground

immigrant A person who has left one country to live in another

professionals Athletes who get paid for playing sports

profits Money left for a business or group after income is collected and expenses are paid

racism Hatred of another race often based on skin color

relief pitcher A baseball pitcher who takes over for another during a game

standardized Made the same; made to agree with a model or rule

tweaked Changed slightly, often to make improvements

vacant Unused, empty space

INDEX